STAIN

Also by Nathalie Anderson:

Following Fred Astaire
Crawlers
Quiver

STAIN

Nathalie Anderson

for Vicki —
compadre !

with respect and love
and ever in solidarity —
Nat

Nathalie M Anderson
May 21, 2018
Swarthmore Honors —

THE HILARY THAM CAPITAL COLLECTION
2017 Selections by Eduardo C. Corral

THE WORD WORKS
WASHINGTON D.C.

First Edition

Stain © 2017 by Nathalie Anderson

ISBN: 978-1-944585-13-6 / LCCN: 2016957979

Acknowledgments

Atlanta Review: "Revelation," International Publication Prize Winner.
Journal of Mythic Arts: "Tell," reprinted in *The Year's Best Fantasy and Horror: Twentieth Annual Collection*.
The New Yorker: "Eh?"
Plume: "Kyoto Without Me."
Runes: "Independence Day."
The Recorder: "Rakushisha," "Shrine," "Stigmata," "The Moon Path," and "World Cup."

"Terra Teratalogica" appeared in *Conscious Mapping: Poets Journey through Verbal Geography*, Rosenbach Museum and Library.
"Green Tea" was commissioned for the retrospective exhibition catalogue *Sarah McEneany*, Institute of Contemporary Art, University of Pennsylvania.
"De Profundis" appeared in *What Writers Do: A Celebration of Lenoir-Rhyne University's Visiting Writers Series*.
"Cathedral" and "The Moon Path" were commissioned for the "Frisson" artists' series at the Columbia S.C. Museum of Art.
Wreckage, with its former title *Secret Heart*, won honorable mention in the University of South Carolina chapbook competition.

I am grateful to Swarthmore College for support in completing this manuscript; and to Abbe Blum, Betsy Bolton, Joy Charlton, Lisa Coffman, Bob FitzSimons, Daisy Fried, Eamon Grennan, Nora Johnson, Nzadi Keita, Kathryn Kirkpatrick, Joan Landis, David Lloyd, Ed Madden, Nina Budabin McQuown, Susan Pearce, Peter Schmidt, Lisa Sewell, Kristina Straub, Elaine Terranova, Eamonn Wall, Lesley Wheeler, Nancy White, Tom Whitman, and Craig Williamson for comfort and advice. And thank you to Eduardo Corral for selecting this book for the Hilary Tham Capital Collection.

CONTENTS

CRUSH

KYOTO

In memory of the mother
gone too early for memory:
Elize Hodges FitzSimons

Even in Kyoto
hearing the cuckoo's cry –
I long for Kyoto.

– Basho
(trans. Robert Hass)

for Abbe Blum

CATHEDRAL

Shade tree, shade tree, shady grove –
the live oak and palmetto –
when summer sun comes lunging
you're glad of any canopy –

even the merest highest cirrus,
even the sheerest sweet-gum leaf
ripped to its ribs and flying.

In the father's house are many mansions –
Japanese magnolia, magnolia grandiflora.
In the mother's house, roof rises over roof,
cathedral nests within cathedral.

*

Wisteria thick-arboring
pergola or verandah –
whatever once comes between you and the sun
will ever shade and shadow you –

even the faintest taint of ginkgo;
even the bruising thumb and fingerprint
of quince, of wincing plum;

or the father's heavy-handedness,
restraining, reassuring;
the mother's black and arching brows,
doors opening onto opening doors.

*

Cloud exalted over cloud,
vaulting the nave and thundering.
The thickening and thickened air
that itched and irked and smothered you.

Your shadow falls down the stair before you,
drags behind you in the street.
For lo, they're ever after with you –

his shuttered eye, her breezy breath,
half bracing, half embracing you –
the leaves of your childhood falling still,
the pecan and the paw-paw.

STAIN

We brake down a great many Pictures superstitious,
20 cherubims,
& the Rayles we brake in peces
and digged down the steps.

— William Dowsing's diary
Swaffham Prior, Cambridgeshire, 1643

STAIN: SIX MEDITATIONS ON THE CRAFT

for stained glass artist Judith Schaechter

"The silver stain," they called it, this medieval innovation –
silver nitrate fired onto glass, turning a white surface
sallow, citron, saffron, sulfur – the silver alchemically
aping gold: a crown, a wing, a head of hair, an apricot
or palomino. No longer did the glazier need to cut
a separate slice of yellow, but could tint and fire and tint again –

as here: a sleeping angel lies,
recently exalted, and exhausted by it,
her wings twitching as a sleeping dog might twitch,
she's that far under – dead to the world,
to the tell-tale apartment, sheets and curtains flung down
over the mattress's sad sags and tuftings, her body haloed
in the spreading, deepening glow
of her own golden piss.

*

Once all this glass was blown by mouth, some in pellucid "muffs,"
        long sleeves
of glass, slit while still warm and ironed flat; some puffed into orbs,
then spun on a rod into circular sheets, "crowns" two feet across
and bulging in the center like a bull's eye. You can tell each type,
however they're sliced, by how the bubbles run: the muff's fine seaming,
the inconspicuous wheels within wheels circling the crown –

as here: beneath the roiling claustrophobic waves
blacking and stropping the top third of this glass
with maelstrom and breaker, heave and viscous spew,
the undersea holds perfectly still its
blank pane of seetheless turquoise

                                        where a girl glides
slantwise silent down, trailing the tug of the rope
of her hair, trailing the drag of the rope
at her heels, trailing the shredded frayed-out played-out rope
of air, that in another century would have held
the caught breath of the blower,
faint spume of last gasps.

                    *

Glass in a slab, a slather of it, what the French call *dalle de verre* –
tilestone, flagstone, pavingstone, stone – like slate laid for a patio,
like marble in a foyer, glass that steadfast, stalwart, sturdy,
glass for building a bridge of air, glass for a staircase up
the slippery slope, glass for Snow White's peekaboo coffin,
fragility forged and thrust and cantilevered into strength –

as here: a veined wing raised up thick, raised up
and out and off, right off
the skin
of the boy
the hive
is stinging.

                    *

Or flash glass: a layer of hue – brilliant, pungent, thunderous –
laid down on a color less extreme, say white glass dipped in red;
or moss shadowed by yew; wine spilled over plum; wisteria
in smoke; peacocks at midnight; lapis over jade – so when scratched
away, the dark layer lightens, softens, cools, quiets, modulates,
and the pale layer – no longer coated, clouded, or benighted – dawns –

as here: flames clawing through the sooted flesh
behind the pyromaniac's back; or here:
the ligature of ligament, the tendon
torqued, the muscle clenched; or
here: the gartered fishnet tugged up, squirmed in, worn
over the bruise, the scab, the open vein; each skin
scraped and abraded, one pain
bolted over another.

*

And *grisaille*: clear glass, white glass, vined and scrolled and interlaced
in black – as here: the widow netted in her veil.

And diapering: an allover patterned background field – as here:
the buttoned quilted cushioned
       walls
padding mad Eva.

And *trompe l'oeil* – the mind says "flower"
though the eye sees "spider"; the mind says "branch"
though the eye sees "oozing"; the mind says "kimono,"
says "languorous," says "pretty," though the eye
sees "dead."

The glass so seductive, so unarguably lovely –
the temptation
to cut and damage –

*

And as for the kid who –
brought up in church –
called saints "people
the Light shines through,"

                all this says yeah, sure, maybe, okay, yes –
but look what it shines through:
look at the stain.

Revelation

Shatterings at Canterbury

If God is a light inaccessible,
a light beyond our comprehension, then
how shall mere eyes see? Pierce our walls
with windows, but shade them, shade them. At Chartres,
light seeps ruby, light pools sapphire. At Sainte Chapelle,
it's dazzling as diamond, all *lux* and *lumen*,
splendor in the glass.
                    If Christ lights the world,
they argued at the time, then his mother
is a window bodying him through, flesh
a translucent shade making the light
bearable. Even so, cathedral on cathedral,
window to window, the sky still blisters
before the Magi, and incandescence
shocks the sleeping shepherds.
                    If God is love
as we've been told, consider well the love
that breaks that glass, window on bright window,
idolatry on idolatry: *Lord,*
what a work was here! What clattering
of glasses! Let the light stream through direct,
they might have said, so every eye can see
God for himself.
                    Thus at Canterbury's shrine
perspicacious rector Richard Culmer,
known to his friends – and this is gospel truth –
as "Blue Dick," climbed *the citie ladder, near*
sixty steps high, with a whole pike in his hand
ratling down proud Becket's glassy bones,
illumination blazing out his eyes.

STIGMATA

Composite Windows, Cambridgeshire

Once the madness passed, who gathered the crazings?
After the schism fractaled into factions,
Seekers grating against Quakers, Ranters rasped
into Baptists, each saintly sect a splinter
rammed under another's skin, how came they in
to the recuperative security
of the secular?
   In the cathedral where
rose windows rose, opened for eternity,
now bared the thorn, now gaped the raw air. Who plucked
each glint off that shout-shivered floor? Consider
the slivers, the slicings, the bloodied hands. Who
harrowed that jigsaw, who grozed those edges clean,
what glazier?
   Watch how those walls kaleidoscope
all we've since gathered of that medieval faith,
the petaling masonry tracing over
an elaborate and deliberate scar,
maintaining, sustaining, reining that lost light.
In utter senselessness, everything moves – who
would have thought it?
    Yes, leaf turns against turret,
red's forced next to blue, tendrils of beard against
a broken crown, swirls of haloed harlot's hair
against a snatch of tonsure, an open hand
slaps up against a fist, elegant feathers
– four torn from a wing – brush past a pleated
gown or smock or swaddled loin. Wheel of fortune,
Catharine's wheel: to each its season. Whose turn?

TYPOLOGY

King's College Chapel

Half an hour's drive from here, in Cambridge,
light's lambent in King's College chapel, light's
wavery like it's glanced off water, light's
rippling and eddying over the choir
as clouds sail by outside. The chapel vault
thrusts ninety feet up to fan itself
and the glass soars with it, twenty-four bays
to south and north, each with ten lights dappling,
five above, five below, the Old Law set
against the New as contrast, as forecast –

Eve yielding thus to Mary; or manna
as foretaste of the Eucharist; Joseph
in his pit evoking Christ in the tomb;
Jonah's loosing from the whale a promise
of the Resurrection – the Old Law reared
to neck-craning height, anticipating
the more forgiving angle of the New.
And all this opulent Renaissance glass
paid for with quick-fallen monasteries:
new faiths, new funds, new finaglings.

*

During the wars, they say, Cromwell readied
his troops here with exercise and parade,
turning and maneuvering them through a space
stripped of all other monuments. They swung pikes
like those thrust against the rebel angels;
they hefted clubs spiked sharp with nails, like those
harrying Christ to Caiaphas. Cromwell,

himself a Cambridge man, looked up to find
unnerving likeness. How the glass escaped
his cleansing, my guidebook does not speculate.

*

But here's the Magdalene, dressed to the nines,
her sandals gold and her stockings muslin,
her dress voluminous with arabesques,
vested in green, skirted in scarlet,
and, here for all to see, her "modesty"
shirred up to her neck, nor any hair
flirting beneath her fancy bonnet, its
floret at the ear, its puff of turban,
its free-floating magenta riband, its
wide brim shading – oh! – her nineteenth century face;

and my favorite, Eve, who's far from eager,
though bare-breasted, tendril-haired, diademed
with pearls, and mirrored in the facing glass
by a bold-faced temptress, *her* hair Titian,
her breast bared too, though she's scarcely naked:
her pelt apple-red and fringed at the hip,
arms daggered so deep they're halfway to wing,
hands clawed and feet clawed, twining her tree, and,
snaking out of nowhere, a tail, supple
and warted and crocodile green, while Eve

is in contrast washed out, a dishwater blonde,
circles stippled weary under her eyes,
her mouth unsmiling as if she's
already sorry, the fruit she holds
her only blush in all that pallor. Eden's
built high behind her – tower, fountain, arch –

while at her feet, up on its haunches, a
lop-eared blue-furred coney, symbol of lust
perhaps, but so unexpected he seems
just the ticket, just my type, good company.

BENEDICITE, OMNIA OPERA DOMINI

St. Mary's, Swaffham Prior, Cambridgeshire

1.

All ye works of the Lord represented,
from Vesuvius (*O ye fire and heat*)
to the Greenland Glacier (*O ice and snow,
O frost and cold*) – and not just simple fact
but fact elaborated: the ice looming wide
and high, dwarfing a lake, a stand of firs;
Vesuvius lipped by waves of lava,
shawled in steam, breached by a flaming beacon;
each scene framed and witnessed by angels, poised
as if holding curtains back, so we see

what God sees: the earth rootless and remote,
alone in the dark or nearly, pale faced
but recognizable from a long way away.
Here winds tug a weathervane (*O ye winds
of God*); here galaxies arc and comets
leap fish-like (*O ye stars of Heaven*); here
lightning blanches the high-clouded sky; here
the nightly owl flees again the morning's lark
(*O ye light and darkness, O ye nights and days,
Praise Him and Magnify Him For Ever*).

And the oceans seething (*O ye whales*) with
shark, seal, porpoise, walrus, nautilus; sky
all float and flutter: hawk, crane, kingfisher,
pheasant, robin, swallow; the hillside stocked
with detached animals (*O all ye beasts*

and cattle); and men, strangely assorted –
Chinese, Eskimo, one labeled "Kaffir,"
a Dyak from Sarawak, the PM
of the Sultan of Borneo (*O ye children,*
children of men) – all circling King Edward;

and – *Bless ye the Lord* – a sunburst eclipsing:
the moon's angled shadow cast down in a sweep
of deep and deeper blue, the green day dusked,
each house and windmill darkened; and – *Praise Him* –
a bit of fen – Wicken Fen – left undrained
at the edge of the fenland, ringed by reed
and reedmace, rush and bulrush, water flag
and water lily, *O all ye green things* –
low sky, high water – *Bless ye the Lord,*
Praise Him and Magnify Him For Ever.

It's clear what Cromwell would make of it – the land he knew
and hoped to mend, lapsed into glass and pagan
with praise; the priests heretically arrayed – Jew, Copt,
Mechizadek, Archbishop, Patriarch, Pope.
Here Nebuchadnezzar turns from his gold idol
quick as any Non-Conformist could desire,
to a God who writes on walls, who walks through flame,
Himself a glass white hot, a window licked wavery
and opening unexpected, for Shadrack,
for Babylon, annealing His believers.

2.

Dedicated at Easter, the springing
of the year, when praise rises ecstatic,
inexorable. And dedicated
when "For Ever" sounded plausible, or
anyhow maybe not yet hyperbolic –
dedicated in the year of our Lord
1914.
      Oh the flames ring them round
like a swirl of hair, roaring red, roaring
yellow, roaring white. How many, think you,
looked to this window for heartening or
for solacing? How many looked on this fire
with mouths twisted and with burnt out eyes?
All ye works of the Lord, Bless ye the Lord,
Praise Him and Magnify Him For Ever.

De Profundis

Memorial Windows
St. Mary's, Swaffham Prior, Cambridgeshire

Whatever would possess a congregation to glass its nave
with armament? Small church, small village, poised at the verge
of the fens, farmers and their sons, dons and dons' daughters –
nothing particularly military round about it. Yet here
at boy's eye height stands a bright boy bugler (*wake up*
the mighty men), and here are women trim as Gibson girls,
those prim long-skirted tennis players, advantageously employed
at packing shells. One window's dedicated to the works of war –

a signal tent, a captured trench (*though they dig into hell*) –
and one is dedicated to war's mitigation – chaplain,
water in the desert, Red Cross van – but both lights rise at last
to weaponry: a howitzer (*the blast is as a storm*
against the wall); rays of liquid fire; a sub and a sub-marine
strewer of mines (*thence will I command the serpent*
and he shall bite); a tin tank, riveted, peculiarly
bobbined (*the man that shall touch them must be fenced in iron*).

Vidimus, medieval glaziers called the sketch stretched out
for the King's approval, a full-sized whitened table or
sturdy pieced-together tablet where the shaped glass
would be laid down, color matched to color, for the joining.
Here is a zeppelin, bone-white by moonlight, convoyed by stars.
Here is the Lusitania, sinking. The terror by night, *vidimus*;
the vapour of smoke, *vidimus*; beneath great waters, among
false brethren – *vidimus, vidimus*: we have seen it.

And here a bi-plane breasts the storm, a picture so appealing
the church sells postcards of it. The clouds it flies are Prussian blue
blustering towards bruise, no angels anywhere in sight. Against that stark
and squalling dark, its snub nose, banty wheels, and paper wings
show bold: wan but willing, spunky, all its struts and pipings
picked out in palest gold. A French-built SPAD, flown by British pilot
and Americans, though here – half-obscured by a cross-bar – the iron cross
brands it as German. "*Though they climb up to heaven*," reads the scripture

chosen for it, "*thence will I bring them down*" – though "safely down"
or "ruthlessly," each one who prays here must decide. *All ye works
of the Lord, Bless ye the Lord*: St. Mary's windows book-end the war,
1914 to 1919, Benediction to Memorial, exuberance to devastation.
There's a third window, too, devoted to peace: springtime and harvest,
green glass and gold glass, the shepherding of sheep. No one talks about it.
Progress, progress, civilization: outside the village, poppies
bleeding through the corn. *Blessed are the dead which die in the Lord.*

Intelligent Design

What was it we believed before we believed
this? That thing with the grape and the grain, that thing
with the wheat and the chaff, that thing with the wine
and the cheese – could they be more sacramental or
transcendental or theologically instrumental, I ask you, than
the blaze in the bush, the blood in the bowl, the bones
in the bearskin, the stones erected so laboriously
or set just so in the raked garden? And is prayer

more efficacious kneeling or prostrate; shaking
or stirred; silent or tongued orgasmic; full-filled
or emptied; facing east or inward; reverencing
some sacred fief or fetish – the figure of a corpse, say,
repeatedly and inventively tortured; or is prayer served better
whirled on a wheel; or flapping its flag in the wind;
scrolled tight between stones; or burnt to black ash; or
tagged onto tin and tipped into the Tiber?
                                    Whatever. Yet

at dawn and dusk, at noon and midnight, counting
the countless galaxies, stars crowding like gnats to the eye, clouds
thick as scales in the scuddings of carp, anyone who looks
can't help but see – that mind so bright, its gaze so sharp – God's
smartening plan: how small we feel, how chosen. Here's an intelligence
we've blinded, still flexing his bow; and here's another, shot full of arrows,
each wound an eye, each eye agape, each mouth of him gasping.
O Zeus-Pater, pierced by Love so mortally and often; O Balder,

sorely wounded by the meekest, softest shaft; O Sebastian,
your head flung back and your eyes starry; and Loki,
sucking back your venom, gnawing down your poisoned darts –
are you my saints, my patrons, each one of you whispering
"give it me"? Though it's late now, isn't it?, for love at first
or second sight, too late for second thoughts, or first thought
best thought. We've felt the edge of that intelligence, found ourselves
pricked by its designs. And before this, what did we know? Was it

eat or be eaten at the gingerbread house? or little blue wolf boys lying dogg
pebbles in the belly and the rusted machete? or broken-toothed babies
bloodying the pillow-slip? or naughty and nice for the whiskered Santa ma
It's been a century and two world wars since Swaffham Prior's
             stained glass master
set its glowing globe in darkest space; and five years now or maybe te
since some local clever-clogs, some crack-shot boy or smart-ass girl
with sling or bow or pellet gun contrived to target it. It hangs there
             by a thread,
our earth, shattered, blasted sharp. Nobody's found the intelligence y
             to mend it.

WRECKAGE

And no way now to know what happened then —
none at all — unless, of course, you improvise.

– Eavan Boland,
"The Black Lace Fan My Mother Gave Me"

*

Improvisations in memory of Elize Hodges FitzSimons

after her photograph album
kept during the Second World War

Secret Heart

I'm not saying it's the only one she kept –
this sooty rustling in the cupboard, this
dessication beating itself off the shelf,
a little tell-tale tattle-tale – yes,
a little tattler, lips sealed to bursting,
tongue held so tight so long it's all one long deep bruise.

Why so mysterious? Against the dark,
exuberance on exuberance: girls
who'd tell all. Friends like sisters; sisters so close
they call each other always only "sister"; a man
grown so familiar, he's wall, he's furniture,
he's shadow; a crowd so tight, who bothers with names?

"Eyes-Only," but the eye's occulted, the eye's
delirious. Not so much hugger as mugger,
not so much cloaked as daggered. Half the time
she marks herself as "X," clips out her own face –
"too awful!" – above the squared off neckline – or
is that someone else's face? I'm not saying

it's the only one she kept, but it's the one
I've got, the beat I learned to beat to –
yes, imperious. I'll pump it hard, I'll
pick its brains, I'll worm it out, I'm
serious: she'll open that chest, she'll
lay it bare, the one she left, left
dark, left in the dark.

Old Home

You know how it is when – after Easter church, because
despite all that solemnity and somnolence the air crisps
with dogwood, and because of course it's no distance, just
down the block, just over the way – the relatives (part
gracious-kind, part mostly oblivious) take the child
through that settled neighborhood to visit the old home – ?

and the grandmother labors and sighs up the walk, up
the steps, that steep hill from the street, and the aunts – girlish
suddenly – giggle and sigh at their porch swing, their Dutch door,
their scuppernongs, their arbored wisteria, the fine net clouding
their windows, their high beds, their sputtering gas jets, yet
for the child there's nothing left of the house, nothing there to see – ?

so it's like a tale of faery, where the balustrade slides
its alabaster slick across the balcony, the floors glide
gleaming, the grand stair rises striding, yet the visitor
wakes to broken twig, trampled moss, spiders in the hair – ?
Materiality has no reality.
She'd have heard that in church, if she'd been listening.

Houses built back from the street, the rise held up, the hill
held back, stone-walled; the neat-faced, neat-dressed, neat-stanced stone
sure-rooted, grown waist high, chest high, where a girl might lean
back on her elbows, might lounge pinafored, saddle-shoed,
her yard a woodland wild with blossom, and her frame house
slatted, dowelled, white washed, welcoming – the kind of house

neglect will grey, turn rickety, turn derelict, the wall
already breached, the stone already broken, the post that's
holding back the break already bitten deep by wire, already
rotted at the root. How can it be immaterial
when it's her one materiality? No matter: every voice
with an O in it. If she walked that street today, she'd lose herself

and never know it.

OLD HAND

I like the way she writes her letter E ~
whether capital or small ~ like an M
tipped to its side ~ top heavy ~ big bosomed ~
a little off kilter ~ a little off key ~

tracing over that letter again and again ~
top curve thick ~ generous ~ bottom curve thinned ~
staining her name on the beige leatherette ~
without scoring the surface ~ without biting in ~

I like this stray red-orange mark ~
a painter's stroke ~ like a scab ~ like a sperm ~
her loopy L ~ her ornate S ~
a little off beat ~ a little off guard ~

I like the button-hook furl at the top of the E ~
the fiddle-head tip of the frond of a fern ~
I like the curlicue kink in its tail ~ as if
the speed of the spiraling curl couldn't quit ~

wingover ~ tailspin ~ fast-falling leaf ~
her name in the air ~ the *Elizee-Bee* ~
a little off hand ~ a little off base ~
E after E after E after E ~

OLD SCHOOL

Teachers larking high-horsed, sweeping majestic down-up-down,
playing at ponies on ponies meant for babies, *whoomp-ah-ah*
the carousel, that little loop in lieu of stirrup lifting the knee
to the withers, lifting the skirt above the knee, the rump
bucked back to the saddle's back, ridged on its ridge line, skirt pleats
pooched out, the sock slouched low in the saddle-shoe, a cowgirl's scarf
flown at the neck, the bloused-out cardigan nipped in at the ribbed waist,
the left hand lifted shoulder-high and waving high-handedly.

Did you think she was maybe waving at you? All of the boys
and all of the girls in Miss Hodges' fifth grade wait and watch
with their hands half-cocked, the pledge of their allegiance, each clutching
their crush, while she rides oblivious, high on her high horse, and
what a horse – a steed fit for Lochinvar! its saddle polished
fifty dozen times a day, its tail a pennon, its mane
a crenellation, and those open-face flowers at bridle
and haunch – roses perhaps, the white and the red – regalia

to blazon and banner about, fit for the boss of a shield,
for the nose of a plane – though she smiling so bright, who would guess
there's a war on? That was the time they all smiled like that – Miss Hodges,
Miss Godfrey, Miss Jennings, Miss Clark – brighter and tighter each day
of the year, waving you in after recess, waving you out
after last bell, waving you home, all the time smiling
not precisely at you, or not at you precisely, their smiles
evidently headed some place else, oblivious alas

to all the ranks of yearning chevaliers. If you'd seen her
with him that Easter, smiling fit to burst – cheeks crab-apple rosy,
crab-apple tight, and dimpled deep to grooves, to gouges; cheeks
squeezed up so high the eyes squinched, the brows bucked, and the hair
rayed out in a cloud from her smiling; wearing buttoned up
over her trim teacher's suit his captain's blouse (its stars, its wings,
its regalia'd glory) – you'd see she'd gone past joust and cheval straight
to bombshell: the precipitous fall, the blinding flash, the wreckage.

OLD FASHION

If I say "girls," you'll see ten-year-olds. If I say "old,"
you'll be imagining their gray hair. But these girls are grown,
if barely grown – grown serious, grown seriously

pleased with themselves. Each girl's hair is parted on the right,
swept back off her face, barretted on the left, but for each
the hairstyle's declarative: Martee's pitch-thick cumulus;

Sarah's clipped ripples and rapids; Julia's waterfall
of elegance, up-turned splash at the end of its drop;
Elize's tiered fountains, spillover and froth. Suited

for the serious face they've chosen, each girl's darkened
and firmed her lips, determined, not quite smiling; has franked
her eyes; looks out from her girlhood steady, reliable,

hirable; each suited up in serge, sure-shouldered,
staunchly double-breasted, necklines equally demure –
the frill, the bow, the pearls, the locket: each difference

declarative. And not just these four: Gusta incisive
in short-sleeved two-piece tailored plaid; Hatsy skeptical
in dark-yoked dark-sleeved black and tan; Carol ever practical,

down on her knees in skirt and stockings, drying her hair
at the heater; or Margaret Jennings, camera slung casual,
steady as Bourke-White in tattersall tweeds, while Elize

scans the test prints, snug sleeves pushed up past her elbows;
or Margaret Allen, in the cinch-waist halter-topped full-skirted
bathing dress Elize wore too, in Florida with Andy; or

that other Margaret, geometric, her sleeves and shoulders
squared off couture-style, smart-edged, exacting, her crossed knee
and Elize's angled off in opposite directions –

mirror girls, the details always declarative,
none of them pin-ups, but with looks that swank
a serious man might take them seriously.

OLD GUARD

They're none of them pin-ups. That's no surprise – and yet
these young men in uniform so court the camera
they might as well be idols of the silver screen: head-shots
handed out like business cards, like calling cards, like
promises, traded among the prettiest girls, pressed
into their prim albums. Take Les Bergum (Wisconsin),

leaning leather-jacketed arms against the wing
of his B-T, his lips just parted as if what he sees
(yes, *you*, the one he's looking at) has left him breathless;
the strut's diagonal shadow – what he looks past
to see you – scored high across his cheek, romantic
as a scar under the dark halo of his captain's cap;

or Theodore McGill, known otherwise as Tater,
"the man who came to dinner": his hair pomaded,
peaked back from his forehead, the comb-lines distinct,
distinctive; leaning forward, urgent, all his brass
catching the light, and a grin so infectious you'd
like to be catching it from him. Even the snapshots glow:

Bill Hall (ΣAE from Mississippi), shirtless
above his khakis, baring tight biceps in a stance
Brando's going to borrow, crouched in the crabgrass, scratching
his spitz behind the ears; or Gene Chewning, clutching
sincerely to his chest his favorite meerschaum, like
he's pledging allegiance or perhaps his heart, honest

and lanky, a Lincolnesque lawyer whose frankness
even Jimmy Stewart's got to envy. The last we see of Gene
he's posing pipe to mouth, playing jaded, playing
the sophisticate, all his angles canted back beneath
a barracks portico so shallow his head's caught
in the raw eaves, some place he doesn't specify

in South America (did you know we shipped our
boys there?), his cocked foot – cocked up, cocked back –
tucked (against propriety and regulation) sockless
into the regulation lace-up. The last we see
of Tater, he's laid up, laid back, playing at bivouac,
playing the man of leisure – box radio, fat cigar –

all his angles netted in a hammock so shallow
his back brushes against the dirt, some place he doesn't specify
in Italy, reading not *Il Popolo* but *The State*,
the Columbia S.C. *State*. The last we see of Bill
(if it's the same Bill), he's back home wearing specs,
his coat too tight for him and fastened too high up, as if

the open-necked shirt and sweater vest weren't enough
to warm him or contain him. The last we see of Les
(if it's the same Les), he looks to have lost fifty pounds,
shrunk back to gawky adolescence, all hunched shoulders
and shadowed eyes; the cartoon stork delivering
with a swift kick a swaddled bomb off the nose of his plane

a kind of unkind likeness; his crew in Sicily,
his crew chief in England as strained as he is; his cheeks
not quite turning up the corners of his smile. And who's this
helmeted GI, his back to the shell-pocked wall, then turned
to face it, so we can see the compact pack he bears,
the holstered canteen riding his hip, the slender rifle

stashed handily just back of his arm, and on his belt
all the little pouches and pockets, his ankles gaitered
over his thick boots, turning his feet to hooves? No one's
had the heart to name him, or these men with their backs turned
marching the dirt road through the wood, the blasted fields:
despite the derring-do, the sturdiness, the urgency,

no way to know who they might have been before, or since become.

OLD FLAME

He's leaning forward, seated, easy, forearms
easy on his knees, seated like a man sits
at a campfire, easy, like a soldier sits
at ease, like a soldier sits abstracted, knees
spread wide, spread lazy, forearms easy on his knees.

The way he sits, he's canopied in forest.
Live oak crowns him, crosses him, and Spanish moss
scrawls over his white t-shirt, shawls his shoulder,
cauls his arm. She's written by his picture, "Not
a cave man," but he's caverned, shadowed, primal,

shuttered, covered, closed; seated like a man sits,
forward, easy; seated like a man sits, closed.
Everywhere else he's clean-cut, dreamy, charming,
dark hair swept back, white bed neatly made,
tie tucked regulation-style, his captain's hat, his wings –

somewhere in Michigan lacing knife-edge ice skates;
somewhere in Texas collaring his dog Butch;
somewhere in Arkansas flying his hand-built
blunt-nosed shark-toothed model bomber; somewhere clasped
buddy-buddy tight and casual by somebody he calls "Doc" –

depths here, maybe cavernous, but he won't cave
though evidently has discovered fire:
a white cloud combing up and charring scorching
between his careful fingers, his out-thrust hands, rapt
as a soldier is, abstracted, easy flare between his knees:

Something he might pilot over the Pacific.
Something to keep dark. Something to let blaze.
Something he might share with her or might not.
Something to fly by. Something that sears.
Lit. Doused. Burnt down. Burnt out. Tarnished.
Half-corroded, oxidized

since maybe 1945.

Old Faithful

Not once seen together, and here's why:
one's always the lens, always picturing the other.
Despite the times, how close they are, these close-ups.
Never a third wheel, third party, third eye.

Where she's crossing that bridge at Cypress Gardens, her mouth sprung
gaping, leaping with laughter, her heel for an instant caught
between planks: he's there at her feet, that dark swathe
of shadow – elbows jutted, steadying; head concentrated, tucked –

his shape an arrow arrowing, a missile fixed, so phallic
you'd laugh too: her shoulder with leafy shade corsaged;
the edge of the bridge darkening his dark, a scarfing;
her coat swayed at the hem from the thought of the thrust of him.

Or here, where she's poised like a pin-up, all frills and espadrilles,
coquettish as heck on the car's hood, lap brimming with sunlight:
he's there at her hip, knowing just where he stands, slim upright
reflected between two stands of trees, back half-arched to the swell

of the fender, though you'll more likely see there the clouded sun
refulgent – the fender's central blaze, the raying off,
the feathering, the sift of cirrus underneath, the gusty puff
of heated cumulus – rather than his reserved refraction.

And where at Red Beach he sits at the surf-line edging the Gulf,
she's the rosy shoal the tide swirls round to reach him.
Were there mirrors, she'd be gracing them, shapely in them.
Were there brass, she'd be the calm cameo.

Or on that dirt road, the late sun stretching her legs long behind her:
he enters the frame from the south east, his eyes aimed for her eyes.
Or sitting by the roadside, her pert suit, her hands loose on her thighs:
he falls for her, falls over her, his shoulder a lap robe, head warming
      her breast.

So when Al Lauf and Bob Korn hunker in the yard
over their own pooled and concentrated darkness, "examining" –
they tell her – "the shadow's teeth," there's bite to their whimsy;
while at that moment, in Guam, in elegant cursives three feet tall,

he names his plane with her name, skies her. All of Tokyo
laid out for her perusal: the prisoners' compound settled on reclaimed earth,
bikes quick as koi in the street along the river's rounded elbow,
      and further north
the angled gables, the flooded fields, the broad and blinding sea, the shadow

of their plane hung over strangeness in the one photo she's up-ended,
turning the world upside down to favor the plane, its head high, wings wide,
soaring. Here the ground's an abstract patchwork, but twist it, and the lines
suddenly turn legible: plowed fields ranged around a homestead,

the furrows meticulous as the roof's ridged tiles; three small branchings –
fruit trees? shade trees? – along the building's sunny side; a vast tree –
camphor? – by the dust-white road; crops well sprouted, leggy, leafy;
a country turning back towards normal, while from this perspective
      the plane's shadow

is blowing over, moving out, headed down. Twenty-two pages,
over two hundred shots, twenty-three of them showing his face,
plus two gone missing – "instructing in Arkansas mud and pine trees";
"flying General Smith to meet the Japanese at Kadena Field" –

not to mention pictures of his quarters, of his model Flying Tiger,
of his dog, his various planes. Twenty-two pages, and then
it ends, it just ends. But thumb through the black at the back of the book:
he's *there*, and he's *there*, and he's *there*, and he's *there*.

OLD SCRATCH

Out of the blue, Al Lauf (New Jersey): the cleft and chiseled chin;
the Eisenhower jacket broadening the shoulder, clipping the waist in;
the parade stance in silhouette – feet together, hands behind –
sharp and steady as a knife blade plunged into the lawn.

On Ascension Island, framed by the tent's dark door, he's all physique,
raising to the eye some sort of scrying instrument; the biceps oblique;
the pyramid that the forearms make shown off by the rolled-up sleeves;
the khakis, even in tropic heat, enviably creased;

and the pistol harnessed to his side a come-on clear to anyone –
though elsewhere he snugs up to his chest his little cocker John;
or stands spread-legged guarding ankle-high hydrangeas, aping Cary Grant;
or in time exposures, too impatient to sit still, clutches a yawning magazine.

Andy's a major now, piloting the *Elizee-Bee*.
Al Lauf – I believe – is a rear gunner, a bombardier.
One of them's on Guam, flying through the last days of the war.
The other's evidently nearer.

Andy leans waving from his cock-pit over eight painted bombs,
each of them tailed by an unclouded star.
Elsewhere, three years to the day before the hour I'll be born,
he sets between his feet – some sort of code? – a little sturdy model horse.

Speculate as you will: wink, or smirk, or frown.
Page after page she merely pastes their pictures down
next to one another, facing one another, shut up tight together, bound,
cleft chin pressed to widow's peak, cheek pressed to jowl.

OLD STORY

1.

I wish I could remember the exact words they said.
Something about a pilot. Something about a plane.
It was after their father's funeral: my aunt Eleanor, my aunt Corinne.
Something about Pearl Harbor. How she broke, hearing he was dead

After their father's funeral, portioning out the albums,
The old grief smashing open, drowning, drowning out the fresher.
Orphaned sisters, orphaned of their sister, missing their orphaned sister,
The names of her friends spicing their mouths, sugary as pecans.

The words they said too sweet for me to swallow.
Portioning out the keepsakes still kept in the chill back bedroom:
A glove-box – her gloves! – scribbled with peacocks. A perfume bottle
Budded girlish with papier maché blooms. And hung on the wall, the photo

I'd never really noticed: plane, ground crew, pilot.
Picture a dropped dinner plate, a shattered water glass.
Heart already broken, what did she give my daddy?
Whatever they said, I couldn't hear, no matter how I listened.

2.

After my father's funeral, portioning out his life,
I find that same photograph – that pilot, that plane,
my mother's name blazoned clear across its sturdy metal –
and the date: August 30th, 1945.

But they'd said – hadn't they? – he died at Pearl Harbor: December 7th, 1941 –
the winter after she finished college, left home: first job, first time on her own.
That's where her album starts. No hint of tragedy.
Rather, surprises: "In a coat at Cypress Gardens"; "Shaw Field in the snow."

I wish I could remember the exact words they said.
By August 30th, the Pacific war is over, the formal surrender
just three days away. Was he downed then? Was she heart-struck?
Maybe he just kept on flying – ? Or maybe she did – ?

Gone past asking, Eleanor, Corinne, my daddy
who spoke of her so rarely, the grief fresh all their long lives.
Like finding in the cupboard a plate, a pristine glass.
Like meeting on the street the youth you thought you left behind.

Old Man

He wanted in the Navy, but knew
he was too slight, so in the rumble seat
of his best friend's Ford, from Columbia to Charleston
he gorged on bananas to bulk out his weight.

He never spoke about the Army,
though men saluted, called him Captain,
and from time to time, from Italy, from France,
letters came, in languages he couldn't read.

Reticence on reticence: skeletons and corpses.
Coins in strange sizes, strange denominations.
Photos set drifting in drawers and boxes.
His portrait in uniform: a face to die for.

And when, precipitous, she left in his keeping
a girl turned three and willful, a boy born only barely,
he spoke of her so softly and so seldom
I'm only just now hearing him.

OLD LINE

So much older, my niece Rachel
graduates this year from Chapel Hill.
She's got her own car, shares a small apartment,
though her daddy still picks up most of the bills.
She's got boys for friends, sometimes boy-friends,
though she doesn't always tell her family their names.
When I open my mother's war-time album,
Rachel's face looks out at me from every page.

And not just hers. Among the photographs of friends
I never met, so close my mother's left them unidentified,
I recognize – I think – her married eldest sister Eleanor
because I see my cousin Vicki's mouth, my cousin Lize's eyes.
And twice she's snapped my grandfather, six years or so before he lost her,
before that sorrow seamed him, bent him, left him frail.
When I look at him in his fit fifties,
I'm shocked to see my little brother there.

                    *

Can "grandmother" be the aptest word
for one who never breathed past thirty?
In these pages, she's always just starting out,
always surprised, outrageous, dewy.
Remember the year you grew from two to three?
I remember not one harsh word, not one
smile, her absence less what I suffer
than simply what I am.

I've got Rachel on my speed-dial,
I've got the album open on my desk,
turning my head from the dead to the living,
from the living back towards the dead.
So much older now – just look at her –
than she ever could be, I –
turned one way or the other –
feel everyday like – finally, today –
I get the chance to meet her.

CRUSH

WORLD CUP

Why do I watch? You're kidding, right? Men, mostly
in their twenties, all of them boyish, all cheekbones
and cheekiness; all of them coltish, canting off
each other in quick canterings; all of them
buckish – their head-butts, their nubbly antlers;
all of them Davids lithe before Goliath

and none of them Goliath – none of them bulked out,
not even Angola, their bullocky shoulders; none
hidebound, not even Germany, so stringently
meticulous; no, none of them bullies – all of them
tendering a hands-up, mussing tenderly the hair
of a man who's just fouled them, a man they've just fouled; or

sending sweetly the ball out when fouls injure
opponents; or stripping off and trading jerseys
after a match fought so foul: the exact same word –
dangerous – for a move that threatens to win or
promises to wound: every man vulnerable, their
heads all unhelmeted, their faces all unguarded,

baring their nationalities as they bare their strong teeth,
jaws just squaring off or sharpening, their grins and flinches
genuine, hair crinkling or crimping or crisping up
in spicules, spit curls, kiss curls; a braid flung heavy
over a shoulder, bangs whipped back from a brow, sweat
sleeked back over a shaving, all of them glistening –

Côte d'Ivoire, clouds coiled tight to their heads, their corn-rows dyed
eye-blue, milk-blue, butte-blue, dune; and Korea, their kicks
high as an animé hero's; and the orange blur
of Holland; the insouciant French *résistance*; Swedes
blond and bristly, fairy-tale princes, solicitous
as Vikings; Spain's Red Fury; Mexico's Aztecas;

and my favorites, Italy, their every man's face
a sketch by Leonardo, their every dancing dash
(or dive) dramatic, histrionic, operatic –
Machiavellian – so when they play Gottuso,
known as the Snarling Dog; and Portugal plays their Pit Bull;
the Dutch their Cannibal; and Ecuador plays Hurt-

ado; Serbia fields Milosevic; and Mexico
their Castro or their Franco, any man among them –
sweeper, keeper, seeker, striker – might serve to demonstrate
how in the heat of combat – menaced or frustrated,
teasing or teased, confused or unlucky, triumphant
or opportunistic – any tousling tussling boy

turns boot, turns brute, turns bruiser, just as long as it takes
for a split-second cleating or clouting: I'm thinking
My Lai; I'm thinking Heditha; and then just like that –
red-faced, red-carded – they're all innocence and outrage
for ninety minutes non-stop: they're genuine, they're masculine,
they're all of them *dangerous*. Of course I watch.

Independence Day

The man in front of me at the fireworks
is rubbing his hands on his girlfriend's back
like he's washing a window. Now that's
no way to treat a dirty girl! I'll bet
he's a big cat, too, when he's kissing her,
sticking his tongue out, all spit and polish,
like he's licking a boot in some army, or
scouring a cone for the last bit
of butter pecan. The girlfriend lingers
her fingers along her brow, so slow
I'm mesmerized, a subtle semaphore –
the way you'd dab at your own lips, or wipe
your own nose, tipping your oblivious friend
to his mustard moustache or his smuts – but
this bozo just scrubs harder. As fireworks
fizzle out there in the night, I watch her
flick her tongue to her own ticklish wrist, like
she's savoring for herself her own
sweet and sour, her own vinegar and salt.

CRUSH

Holding hands tight through the crowded museum,
Among the blue Picassos she started to fall.
Her foot lodged against his foot, arm to arm extended:
A tango turn. She went down graceful.

"Let her down easy." Any one of us would tell him so.
The crush shrank, rippled back, water from a stone.
Deep swimmer, deep swimmer: her hair pooled around her.
Under that water, she kept her eyes open.

She lay as she fell, landfall or deadfall.
We looked for her face, but no one was in.
Around her, our headphones kept up their susurrations.
Some were saying *relay*, some *ship*, some *shun*.

Walls tilting in, room turning about her.
Gold leaf splintering: that weight off her chest.
We could feel it ourselves: the whirlpool, the crush,
Clouds whipping round. Still holding her hand.

PREDICTABLE

The fortune-teller flat out told me I
wouldn't be happily having you
on this or any other life line.

In the heart of the heart of the Pink Rose Café
exactly where the pistils and the stamens ought to be,
our chair backs that wiry, that tremulous and high,

I held my hands out, beseeching,
over pastry pollen, shortbread grit,
nakedly weighting the fly-away cloth

down to the slick formica, the table tipsy
except for my utter gravity, the walls around us
fluttery as petals light's passing through. He

turned me palm up, palm down, up again,
scored me with his thumbnail, marking how
I'd go straight on without you, though shaken so

I felt the lines were blurring. He stroked my damp palm
not unkindly, before he wrung your name right out of it,
watched you seep entirely away. The teacups

rattled in their saucers. *Keep your hands
to yourself,* time after time he warned me,
and you did too, but I'm not persuaded.

EH?

Eh he said and she
dreamed eh. It was
like that between them.

Not that his lips dreamed,
not that his dreamed lips
parted. Eh he'd say

and her dream was eh,
was all eh, all and
only. Sometimes

a near kiss an almost tide
drawn back withdrawn withdrawing.
Sometimes the hackled wave

raised, drew back its lip, sheered
its teeth, coughed its raw
guttural. Or

she herself voicing
involuntary *eh*
his whatever, his

what-it-is. But
sometimes his naked eh
with her ah alongside –

the rocked hulls nudging nuzzling
or was it scraping what
did she care? Would his eh

oh? How fast she'd
founder, taking on water,
mouth emptying full.

By day she'd hear on the air
his syllable, turn
toward or away, does it

matter? If she said ah
would he dream ah? Oh –
not like that between them.

The Moon Path

After a painting by Elliott Daingerfield,
Columbia Museum of Art, Columbia, S.C.

It was on the moon path where I last denied him,
where moonlight gloved the hand he raised in parting, slicked
the side of his face, brightened his white hair. I see now,
he said: I'm no one's dream or future. It was

just days since he died, but still it took me long enough
to work through the pun of it, his double-edged and
two-faced implication, while he paused a moment
in the ivory doorway, letting it all go. I wonder

how I looked to him then, my throat tight and my hands
clenching, the veil of moonlight cast over my face,
my flesh pearling with it, shawled with it, light whirling
me round like a garment in wind, rippling the leaves

into waves so I walked like the moon on that water –
how any girl looks to the eyes he sees with now.
In my dreams, even still, he's always propositioning.
In his, it was always proposing.

DINNER WITH SATYR

At first brush it's attractive, how
he concentrates his air, watching
and not watching, rapt and raptor –
might snort you or snore you, might spring
any which way, not seeing who
or even where you are, snuffed up
in the *what* of you, savory
consumable. Delicious, too,

at first brush that rap-tap on arm
chest cheek shoulder, yours or his own
scarcely matters, available
surface idle enough to ground
his sparking heartbeat, its shock so
rare and erratic only he
can dance to it: his various
swoops and leapings, sure-footed

over precarious rocks or
logics, perked ears thick thicketed
in carefully careless haircut,
massive shakings of the massive
hair and head. Tasty, too, how Beast
loves Beauty, dotes on it, smitten –
grazing and fondling and nuzzling
without ever quite touching

your host's dearest daughter. Was he
soused on arrival? He's soused now,
has downed every dram of your host's
pecan brandy, all come-hither
side glance, all saltings and drippings.
Beauty passes the gravy, moves
down the table, away from his
lippy leanings, his

sticky-fingered ravenous
profundities. Not to worry.
Any time now, he'll start flaying
himself: knows he's no Apollo –
though wince-thin Parisians crave him
to the giblets, as he'll soon rap-tap
blurt-blab to the *what* of you. Yes,
you'll dine out on this one a long time.

Terra Teratalogica

After a map of the known world, 1543.

My Dearest Doctor Dee: If it's not one Thing
it'll be another. North, at the curling lip
of the *Mare Congelatum*, the frozen sea,
it's Anthropophagi, who'd as soon swallow you
as talk with you at table. South, where the mountains

sweat to float the Nile, it's Troglodytae, cave-things, wild
to bury you. *Terra es, terram ibis*: you're dirt to them;
they'll speed to spade you under. Go East? The worms they raise
in Sym and Seres sup on forests, bolt men whole.
And in the West, the honeyed lands? Doctor, consider the bees.

By sea, no safer. Off Madagascar it's Gorgones.
Elsewhere a mapmaker, at a loss for proper names, looks
to sketch the danger: sinuous seas looped and knotted, ships
gripped to the rigging, oceans reared up badger-faced and
spewing oceans. Earth shakes. Ships sink. No such thing

as *terra firma*. Still, my invitation stands. Are you
with me, Doctor Dee? The towering twinned columns
of Alexandria are fallen, the altars of Caesar
overturned. In Arabia Deserta – steeped so deep
in incense once, they called it "*felix*," happy – the sands hunch now

like great cats, slink and pounce like cats, watch – *ocelis* – with cats' eyes.
Even the kittens bare their claws. When the hand of every Thing
is turned against you, it's no time to show your own hand. That's why
I live in *terra incognita*, where every bush
is bladed, every coast is cleared, and every strange Thing

held at bay. I urge you, Doctor: leave Samara on the Volga, leave
Samarra on the Tigris, leave Samartia on the Black Sea, leave
Samaria and Samarkand behind. Here, what we have is
newer, cleaner, emptier. See for yourself: my door
is open for you; my house is your house; my *terra*

is your *terra*.

TELL

One sees. One is enticed. One goes
or not. One pines, or not. That's all
it is. Still, every time one tells,
by hairsbreadth, hairsbreadth, on it grows.

The slant of eye. The cut of tooth.
One thinks what one describes explains.
While spouses sneer and parents strain,
sift sigh from sly, clip rune from brood.

Whatever one might think to say
one says. Despite one's innocence
strange words serve, stranger, to estrange.
Hearsay. Soothsay. Verité. Fey.
One's wooden tongue sprouts eloquence.
Oh changeling, this is how you change.

TROLL

Troll under her bridge, raw from clawing up
her rankling, swollen green with grudgery,
feeling on her spine each splintery plank,
each trip trap tramp, each neat little goat's hoof.
She's a cat-fit rash for rocketing, back
always up, hackles always bristling. She's
the worm in your apple, thorn in your flesh.

When troll meets troll at day's end, what ecstasies
of grumbling. Says this: "One drove before me
gratingly slow, and the last parking place
filched thievishly. Had the gall to ask then
for directions: TROLL FACE! TROLL FACE! One
won't ask again. I'm the fly in your ointment,
snake in your grass, skeleton at your feast."

"Uh-huh," says that: "I've claimed my window seat
when two come giggling, want seats together,
want me to trade: TROLL TONGUE! TROLL TONGUE! Two
won't ask again. I'm the stick in your craw, boil
on your backside, edge on your teeth." "Uh-huh,"
says this: TROLL FIST! "Uh-huh," says that: TROLL FANG!
Back and forth the bad blood, the belly-aching.

And where do they get off, those billy-goats,
calling themselves gruff? Here they come again,
traipsing so innocent, with their butt-heads,
their daggers, their bull-dozer shoulders. Ha!
Dunk her or drown her, she pops right back up
with her havoc and hoodoo. She's the mange
in your manger, iceberg in your bath.

She's your nil wind. She's your own weevil star.

KYOTO

OLD VIEWS

If it were me, today, in my own tin plane,
I'd be looking for temples, I'd be looking
for castles, I'd be looking for Fuji.
At the time, even after the truce, he saw

only targets: the hook of a harbor, the sight line
raised by a tower, the T where an island
allows three bridges, the X where one road
crosses another. They've re-built Tokyo

two dozen times since then, even the well-nigh
eternal landmarks – river, port – long since crowded
out of sight. Looking over the plane's left shoulder
beyond the origami folds and flaps the wing makes

as it readies to descend, I see the rice fields
brim with twilight, the subtle slope of their
silvering enclosures like an extension
of the wing. "No friend of mine," he's written –

someone's written – on the photo of a field
back home, its scarecrow contrived to look, to seem, somehow
Japanese – the brimless straw hat tugged down helmet-style,
low to the ear, low to the brow; the armless shirt

compacting and sturdying the torso; the broom-backed
flat-shouldered stance somehow – uh huh –
un-American, despite the rolled-up
clay-heavy dungarees. Hard to believe, today,

a bird would fly from anything so static –
though seems like at the time that stunted icon
could make anything take fright. Times change: now, how
home-spun, how ragged seems the scarecrow. After the truce, he flew

to snap each monument, each property, each land line
or sea lane that, just the day before, he aimed
to obliterate: snaps, snaps up, takes, keepsakes, his
for keeps. They've rebuilt Tokyo, but –

road for road, roof for furrow, sprig
for sprig – every farm north of the city looks
precisely the same. You'll have to take my word for it:
sighting over the plane's left shoulder, I forget

to raise my camera, forget to take the shot,
with what he saw so clear in black and white some
sixty years gone, rising up to meet me
in soft folds of saturated green.

Koi

At Heian-ji, they
rise as one, brisk
hailstorm pocking
the pond's skin
from within – placidly
plosive, plosively placid.

At Rakusho, it's
huddle and scrum, it's sizzle
and spank, it's spurt and scud. Where
water's racing, the turn-tail bolt,
sluicing skirmish, roister
and ruckus, the slip-stream
scrimmage.

At Koko-en, a run of stitches
pulls through the silk, pleating
the waters. Straight seams.
Sliced peach, sliced apricot –
kites on a string,
processionals.

At Maruyama-koen, the heron
meditates, rapt
raptor. In the impassive pond, a splash
of reflective azalea
curves like diving koi.

Is it sunset, or sunrise?
At Tenryu-ji – red here, white there – they
bobble the water: ripple
crosses ripple, shimmers both ways.

SHISEN-DO

For every slightest quaking leaf, a gardener
to lull and hush it. For every flighty gust of green,
a gardener to sleek it, clip the wing. For every spree
of branching limb, a gardener to rein it, bend
back the wrist, twist the arm in. No sprig evades
their blading, no frond their fondest scrutiny.

Comes one in cloth boots, so not to mar the mosses.
Comes one in cloth hands, so not to bark or bruise.
Comes one in a hat sloped like a hillock, the eye
tented always to the task. Comes the calipers,
the secateurs. And one with a twig broom, whisking
back into air the falling rain. It's here

I learn from my companions their proper names
for azalea, iris, maple – the neighborly plants
of my childhood, plants I clearly only thought I knew.
I bow, bow lower. Gardeners, quick in their cadres,
pluck and plump the plush green pillows, silent
wire-pullers, harrowers, the hidden hand, the henchmen –

fit hierophants for this House of the Immortals, papered
with poems pruned back to the bud, pruned back
to the branching. Listen. A bamboo pipe gulps,
swallows its mouthful, balances, balances, falls
with the weight, then gulps again, its slow sips
and sudden slaps a gentle feint to scare away the deer.

Rakushisha

Poet's Hut
House of Fallen Persimmons

So quick, the cloud flung
over the garden, trailing
its beaded fringe, that
delicate pelting.

Under the thunder,
falling suns, their heft
explosive, stormed to bursting:
coronas of succulence.

And then the moon,
all pocks and rots and bruisings.
It softens on my window sill:
ghost fruit.

Karesansui: Dry Gardens

Kodai-ji, Nanzen-ji, Ginkaku-ji,
Ryogen-in, Daisen-in, Ryoan-ji

As if a pool
caught itself
caught itself up
rain plucking into it

As if a stream
outran itself
ran itself short
frayed itself to tatters

As if a mist
muscled into its river
rifts turning mid-current
pelt beading up thick

As if a waterfall
fell hard for you
granite cataracts
dust smoldering

As if a lake
threw up its hands
flung out its arms
its deep-sunk embrace

As if a sea
calmed itself
laid down its waves
fingers through its curls

As if a moss
combed up and troughed
ground swells tipped
with coral foam

Grain by grain, the sand
declines each night
its raking,
abstracted again

Abstract it again

Stone flows
Earth eddies
A single fern frond
trembling

Zen Banquet

1.

A single leaf – shiso –
battered, blazed

    – yes, tempuraed –

        on one face only

the green side greener,
its ribs looser, more expansive
      for the other side's quick
crisps and clutchings

the turn of season
      made audible
      made edible.

2.

Ribbons of eelskin
eased from the eel

into boiling seas

the kinking up
the cinching

     string for a missing finger
     mouthful
         for the tongue-tied.

3.

My Seven-Course Meal at Okutan:

First, tofu "sesame":   licked slick with it
                                 the three wee seeds
                                 two scathings of scallion

Second, tofu "sushi":   white bedded in white
                                 pillows
                                 and the summer coverlet

Third, tofu "wasabi":   faint filings
                                 fallen cryptic –
                                 ghost-green *hiragana*

Fourth, tofu "tempura":   sun-stroked,
                                 melting
                                 in crinkled kimono

Then tofu soup: twinge of turnip
                                 tangent of pumpkin
                                 gilded lily

Last: five clean white tiles
                                 washed bright
                                 in mountain water

And after: skewered twice, grilled on those sticks
               slipped slapped slopped
               with sea-sweet bean paste

                         Yes, even the glaze
                         another guise.

CLOSE ENCOUNTERS:
TWELVE BRIEF ILLUMINATIONS

After showering, I see myself as Samurai –
hair raked back from teeth-bared stare. Now
who'll talk to me?

*

Bangs drip, brows drip, downpours – less women
than waterfalls wading the Philosopher's Path,
we stream past each other, each philosophical.

*

Temple lecturer,
packed treasure house. For an hour,
wordless, I follow his hands.

*

Nara: twelve twelve-year-olds each ask
"You like Japan?" I stutter my *hai*s.
"You work hard," one says.

*

Worshippers at Chion-in: torsos
upright, so strenuous they
look to be standing.

*

Or prostrate. Incense,
singing floors. She settles back
into the cradle of her heels.

*

At the procession – Aoi Matsuri – American students
jostle, point, squeal, flirt, back-bite. Japanese
apologize to one another. For them!

*

Pickles she's made with her own hands,
nine kinds: stem, root, flesh, fruit, flower. For each
my guidebook says, "ginger."

*

Toddler toddles headlong through the temple, breaks
breakneck for the chiming priest.
Overshadowed, the mother bows and bows.

*

Ryoan-ji: serene, I buy
zen postcards. Monks push past,
swaggering, clattering.

*

At the exhibition, poets among photographs, she and I
mime *focus, pinhole, long exposure* –
wordless, visionary, high.

*

And philosophical: two women our age make
strange strangers, nod as we pass, eyes
crinkling, smiles wry.

Green Tea

After a painting by Sarah McEneany

Raised dais, intimate alcove –
like every bath, a privy shrine where you're
the icon, white-walled, incognito.

Tile replicating tile –
a graph, a fever chart where you're
the fever, flush-faced, almost spiking.

The rug rucked up a bit
and rippling. Say ah. Stick out your
roughened tongue. Antiseptic? Sybaritic?

*

Bit of water. Bigger bit of water.
Hiss in the pipes. A spritz. A hiccup.
Tides rise and fall: your half-moon face.

The slap of hot. The bite of cold.
A drop. A drip. A drizzle
drenched daughter, hair dunked and drifting.

Saint stripped to essence,
waisted in water,
that see-through swirling skirt.

*

Heather, hyssop, hickory, hibiscus –
cleft stick, split seed, splinter, fissure.
The brittle leaf. The leaf gone shattery.

Willow, linden, myrtle, thistle.
The macerated twig. The severed tendril.
Good strong tea. The mince medicinal.

Whin, fig, ginseng, eucalyptus.
Crisp frond whisked with skeletal petal.
Bitter herbs: the whole caboodle.

                    *

A woman in hot water, hot
and bitter water, the woman
steaming, the water seething green

and leafing. White tiles
blush, warm, soften,
mist moistening the towel's tongue.

A tippler topping up the cup.
A woman brewing. Yes, hot stuff,
steeping yourself in porcelain.

KYOTO, WITHOUT ME

chills and goes dark. At this very instant
even the Gion district – its silk suits, its draggled
dragon-kimono drag – blows out, blows shut

and a hostess hesitates mid-gateway,
not sure what she's missing, thinking to lift
from its chest again the quilted antique jacket.

Here, autumn falls hard. Trees bare their bones and
the winds rake through them. Leaves shiver the streets,
shrinking from umber down into dun. There –

bronze over ochre, ochre over gold,
each garden's lanterned by the flickering:
full-moon maple, dancing-peacock maple –

or would be, were I there to see it. Where
at highest noon in the furthest reaches
of Maruyami Park, one man only

passed me striding, and one man only
passed me sighing, where the ghost fern curls
to the finger pool, and the moss deepens,

at this very instant, does anyone linger,
bereft of even the sickle moon,
unaware that it's me that he's missing?

Shrine

1.

Perhaps because I dropped in the box
only my smallest coins – the weightless ones,
dull as tarnish, worth at the time well less
than a hundredth of a hundredth – the bell,

for me, would not sound. I grasped the rope,
tugged it and twisted it, hurled it about
like a lariat, but for me the bell
did not answer. For the woman before me, yes,

with her bowed head. For the children behind me,
yes, for all their giggling. "Go, litel bok," I said,
because that's every poet's prayer, but for me
the bell gave no reply. The fox on the left

with the key in his jaws did not drop it,
did not loosen his grip, not even to grin. And
when I spread there a handful of *ume* –
dried plums, fruit favored by foxes – perhaps because I

held back for myself the bulk of the packet,
the bell spoke not a word. The fox on the right,
his muzzle closed on succulence, found nothing
I could offer him more tempting to his bite.

2.

One after one, *torii* on *torii*,
the red gates usher the petitioner,
so slender they're no shelter. Rain falls
and leaves fall between those gates; beyond them
the stream calls, the birds call. There's no combing
of sands or of grasses, no gathering up
of fallen leaves or branches, the trees so dense
no one would dare to cut them. To meet a fox
in all that twilight, where they toss about
their prey? Bound with straw ropes, the trees surge up,
swell out, press thick against their bondage, the leaves glistening,
the paths glistening, the breath so deep in the throat
in the chest, oh more, drink more of it, glistening.
"Go, litel bok," I said, but I can't say
if it was listening, out there among the foxes.

Notes

CATHEDRAL: After Nade Haley's airy installation "Homage to Abbott Suger," Columbia Museum of Art, Columbia S.C.

STAIN:

Works I've consulted in writing this sequence include:
  The Book of Common Prayer…of the Protestant Episcopal Church,1952.
  Michael Camille, *Gothic Art: Glorious Visions*.
  Elisabeth Everitt and Roy Tricker, *Swaffham-Two-Churches: A Guided Stroll Through the History of the Churches of St Mary the Virgin and of St Cyriac and St Julitta in Swaffham Prior in the County of Cambridgeshire*.
  John Harries, *Discovering Stained Glass*, a Shire guide revised and expanded by Carola Hicks.
  Claire Oliver, *Judith Schaechter: Selected Works 1988-2003*, Claire Oliver Gallery.
  Extra Virgin: The Stained Glass of Judith Schaechter, foreword by Alex Baker, Free News Projects & Lawrene Publications.
  Judith Schaechter's website, www.missioncreep.com/schaechter
  Judith Tannenbaum, *Heart Attacks: Judith Schaechter*, with essays by Rick Moody and Maria Porges, Institute of Contemporary Art, Philadelphia.
  Josephine Warrior, *King's College Chapel* guidebook, with photographs by Tim Rawle and James Austen.
  Hilary Wayment, *King's College Chapel, Cambridge: The Great Windows, Introduction and Guide*.

I am particularly indebted to these authors for the following:
  From "Parables in Glass," a statement by Judith Schaechter found on her website: "Another major reason I stick with stained glass is because I think the raw material is pretty. The

uncut sheets of colored glass are really seductive, awesome, and unarguably lovely things. Naturally, the temptation to cut and damage all that pristine beauty is too much for me to resist."

In *Gothic Art*, Camille reviews "the theology of Pseudo-Dionysius, a supposed fifth-century Christian mystic whose ideas about God as an 'incomprehensible and inaccessible light' were revived in the twelfth century." Camille also distinguishes various forms of light as defined by medieval theologians – *lux* (a luminous source like the sun), *lumen* ("light multiplied in space"), and *splendor* ("light reflected off objects"); he develops the idea that the Virgin Mary "is the 'window of heaven,' the *fenestra coeli*, 'through which God shed the true light on the world'"; he traces the shift from the "opaque, almost dark, mystery" embodied in the stained glass at Chartres to the more transparent and refractive glass represented by Sainte Chapelle; and, in an analysis of Taddeo Gaddi's paintings for the Baroncelli Chapel at Santa Croce, Florence, notes the "incandescent flash of light [that] shocks the shepherds from their sleep."

"Lord, what a work was here!" comes from the diary of William Dowsing, who stripped the churches of East Anglia of superstitious ornament during Cromwell's depredations; quoted in Harries & Hicks. Richard "Blue Dick" Culmer, the rector of Chartham in Kent, was responsible for "cleansing" Canterbury Cathedral during Cromwell's campaign, also in Harries & Hicks: "One July Sunday 'during divine service the lightning fell upon the spire … a ball of fire descended into the body of the church and burst in the middle aile with a most violent explosion.' This was taken as a bad omen…."; "On January 3rd [1643] at Swaffham Prior, Dowsing's diary records that 'we brake down a great many Pictures superstitious, 20 cherubims, & the Rayles we brake in peces and digged down the steps.' The word 'Pictures' in Dowsing's vocabulary often denotes stained glass." Quoted in Everitt and Tricker.

WRECKAGE:

During the Second World War, before she ever met my father, my mother kept an album of photographs cataloguing her activities. It's a happy album, hinting at flirtations and madcap doings, until suddenly it stops cold. As with most such personal artifacts, it keeps its secrets.

After graduating from Lander College in 1941, my mother worked as a fifth grade teacher in Florence, S. C., near Shaw Air Force Base. Most of the young women pictured in her album are probably friends from Greenwood, S.C., her hometown, working with her in Florence. Most of the young men are evidently pilots.

Peppered through the album are pictures of a man identified only by his first name, Andy; among its last pages are photographs he's sent her from Guam, dated August 1945. Who he was, what he meant to her, what happened to him: never specified.

She married my father in 1947; I was born in 1948; and three years later, when she was thirty, my mother died, of complications in a second pregnancy. Some fifty years later, after my father's death, the album came to me.

SECRET HEART echoes Rod Stewart's song of that name.

TERRA TERATOLOGICA: After Caius Julius Solinus: *C. Iulii Solini Polyhistor, Rerum Toto Orbe Memorabilium thesaurus locupletissimus*, Basel, 1543.

Terra es, terram ibis: "Dust thou art, to dust thou shalt return."

ZEN BANQUET: MY SEVEN-COURSE MEAL AT OKUTAN: In my favorite *New Yorker* cartoon (by Warren Miller, June 15, 1981), the wife bears to the board a whole roast pig, spiced apple sweetening its mouth, its trotters splayed, its tail crimped tight, circled by spuds and garnishes and all the fixings. Husband, unimpressed, can't help but whine, "Tofu, in yet another guise?"

About the Author

Nathalie Anderson's first book, *Following Fred Astaire*, won the 1998 Washington Prize from The Word Works; her second, *Crawlers*, received the 2005 McGovern Prize from Ashland Poetry Press; and her third, *Quiver*, was published in 2011 by Penstroke Press. Her poems have appeared in such journals as *Atlanta Review*, *DoubleTake*, *Natural Bridge*, *The New Yorker*, and *The Recorder*; they're included in *The Book of Irish American Poetry From the Eighteenth Century to the Present* (Notre Dame); and have twice been solicited for inclusion in *The Year's Best Fantasy and Horror* (St.Martin's). She has authored libretti for four operas – *The Black Swan*; *Sukey in the Dark*; an operatic version of Arthur Conan Doyle's *A Scandal in Bohemia*; and a children's opera, *The Royal Singer* – in collaboration with the composer Thomas Whitman. A chapbook of her poems exploring a debt between the races in pre-Civil War Charleston S.C. – *Held and Firmly Bound* – will be published by Muddy Ford Press in 2017. A 1993 Pew Fellow, Anderson serves as Poet in Residence at the Rosenbach Museum and Library in Philadelphia, and she teaches at Swarthmore College, where she serves as the Alexander Griswold Cummins Professor of English Literature and directs the Program in Creative Writing.

THE HILARY THAM CAPITAL COLLECTION

Nathalie Anderson, *Stain*
Mel Belin, *Flesh That Was Chrysalis*
Carrie Bennett, *The Land Is a Painted Thing*
Doris Brody, *Judging the Distance*
Sarah Browning, *Whiskey in the Garden of Eden*
Grace Cavalieri, *Pinecrest Rest Haven*
Cheryl Clarke, *By My Precise Haircut*
Christopher Conlon, *Gilbert and Garbo in Love*
    & *Mary Falls: Requiem for Mrs. Surratt*
Donna Denizé, *Broken like Job*
W. Perry Epes, *Nothing Happened*
David Eye, *Seed*
Bernadette Geyer, *The Scabbard of Her Throat*
Barbara G. S. Hagerty, *Twinzilla*
James Hopkins, *Eight Pale Women*
Brandon Johnson, *Love's Skin*
Marilyn McCabe, *Perpetual Motion*
Judith McCombs, *The Habit of Fire*
James McEwen, *Snake Country*
Miles David Moore, *The Bears of Paris*
    & *Rollercoaster*
Kathi Morrison-Taylor, *By the Nest*
Tera Vale Ragan, *Reading the Ground*
Michael Shaffner, *The Good Opinion of Squirrels*
Maria Terrone, *The Bodies We Were Loaned*
Hilary Tham, *Bad Names for Women*
    & *Counting*
Barbara Louise Ungar, *Charlotte Brontë, You Ruined My Life*
    & *Immortal Medusa*
Jonathan Vaile, *Blue Cowboy*
Rosemary Winslow, *Green Bodies*
Michele Wolf, *Immersion*
Joe Zealberg, *Covalence*

THE WASHINGTON PRIZE

Nathalie F. Anderson, *Following Fred Astaire*, 1998

Michael Atkinson, *One Hundred Children Waiting for a Train*, 2001

Molly Bashaw, *The Whole Field Still Moving Inside It*, 2013

Carrie Bennett, *biography of water*, 2004

Peter Blair, *Last Heat*, 1999

John Bradley, *Love-in-Idleness: The Poetry of Roberto Zingarello*, 1995, 2nd edition 2014

Christopher Bursk, *The Way Water Rubs Stone*, 1988

Richard Carr, *Ace*, 2008

Jamison Crabtree, *Rel[AM]ent*, 2014

Jessica Cuello, *Hunt*, 2016

B. K. Fischer, *St. Rage's Vault*, 2012

Linda Lee Harper, *Toward Desire*, 1995

Ann Rae Jonas, *A Diamond Is Hard But Not Tough*, 1997

Frannie Lindsay, *Mayweed*, 2009

Richard Lyons, *Fleur Carnivore*, 2005

Elaine Magarrell, *Blameless Lives*, 1991

Fred Marchant, *Tipping Point*, 1993, 2nd edition 2013

Ron Mohring, *Survivable World*, 2003

Barbara Moore, *Farewell to the Body*, 1990

Brad Richard, *Motion Studies*, 2010

Jay Rogoff, *The Cutoff*, 1994

Prartho Sereno, *Call from Paris*, 2007, 2nd edition 2013

Enid Shomer, *Stalking the Florida Panther*, 1987

John Surowiecki, *The Hat City After Men Stopped Wearing Hats*, 2006

Miles Waggener, *Phoenix Suites*, 2002

Charlotte Warren, *Gandhi's Lap*, 2000

Mike White, *How to Make a Bird with Two Hands*, 2011

Nancy White, *Sun, Moon, Salt*, 1992, 2nd edition 2010

George Young, *Spinoza's Mouse*, 1996

THE TENTH GATE PRIZE

Jennifer Barber, *Works on Paper*, 2015
Roger Sedarat, *Haji as Puppet*, 2016
Lisa Sewell, *Impossible Object*, 2014

OTHER WORD WORKS BOOKS

Annik Adey-Babinski, *Okay Cool No Smoking Love Pony*
Karren L. Alenier, *Wandering on the Outside*
Karren L. Alenier, ed., *Whose Woods These Are*
Christopher Bursk, ed., *Cool Fire*
Barbara Goldberg, *Berta Broadfoot and Pepin the Short*
Frannie Lindsay, *If Mercy*
Elaine Maggarrell, *The Madness of Chefs*
Marilyn McCabe, *Glass Factory*
Ann Pelletier, *Letter That Never*
Ayaz Pirani, *Happy You Are Here*
W. T. Pfefferle, *My Coolest Shirt*
Jacklyn Potter, Dwaine Rieves, Gary Stein, eds., *Cabin Fever: Poets at Joaquin Miller's Cabin*
Robert Sargent, *Aspects of a Southern Story & A Woman from Memphis*
Fritz Ward, *Tsunami Diorama*
Amber West, *Hen & God*
Nancy White, ed., *Word for Word*

INTERNATIONAL EDITIONS

Kajal Ahmad (Alana Marie Levinson-LaBrosse, Mewan Nahro Said Sofi, and Darya Abdul-Karim Ali Najin, trans., with Barbara Goldberg), *Handful of Salt*

Keyne Cheshire (trans.), *Murder at Jagged Rock: A Tragedy by Sophocles*

Jean Cocteau (Mary-Sherman Willis, trans.), *Grace Notes*

Yoko Danno & James C. Hopkins, *The Blue Door*

Moshe Dor, Barbara Goldberg, Giora Leshem, eds., *The Stones Remember: Native Israeli Poets*

Moshe Dor (Barbara Goldberg, trans.), *Scorched by the Sun*

Lee Sang (Myong-Hee Kim, trans.), *Crow's Eye View: The Infamy of Lee Sang, Korean Poet*

Vladimir Levchev (Henry Taylor, trans.), *Black Book of the Endangered Species*

CPSIA information can be obtained
at www.ICGtesting.com
Printed in the USA
BVOW03s0502210217
476732BV00001B/1/P